Paens

Ashley Crystal Lili Bueche

Order this book online at www.trafford.com
or email orders@trafford.com

Most Trafford titles are also available at major online book retailers.

Printed in Victoria, BC, Canada.

ISBN: 978-1-4269-2502-3 (sc)
ISBN: 978-1-4269-2503-0 (hc)

Library of Congress Control Number: 2009913682

*Our mission is to efficiently provide the world's finest, most comprehensive book publishing
service, enabling every author to experience success. To find out how to publish your book, your
way, and have it available worldwide, visit us online at www.trafford.com*

Trafford rev. 03/30/10

www.trafford.com

North America & international
toll-free: 1 888 232 4444 (USA & Canada)
phone: 250 383 6864 ♦ fax: 812 355 4082

To my 6th grade English teacher, Mrs. Dauber for feeding my brain brazil nuts and classical music as my mind's eye sought poetry for salvation. And to my old friend Eric Crimson, for without your kind friendship and beautiful heart I would have never found the strength to survive and seek my dreams come true.

"*All* that we or seem
Is but a dream within a dream."

Edgar Allan Poe

Contents

Preface

Welcome to my mind's eye, a sliver of a chapter in my past. In the following pages you will bear witness to my torments, my illusions, my faults, my cares and loves, my truths, my observations in a paradise garden. Broken dreams and distilled fears I drifted into oblivion far into the depths of twilight. With a few letters painted on a blank canvas, I have created this out of chipped ashes of the mold that was once me, that is still me. This is not a mini series but a volume of many more to come as long as I shall feel and think. Here today, gone tomorrow. Carpe diem my darlings.

The Garden Needs Watering

Ay I sulk once more in the faint
quaint sound of petals dropping

Woe I have seen

The ashes burn still

Plushes of fog soothe the

Unrestly tidal waves

Five fingers, one way

One after the other my thoughts
Rumble and intertwine

The chamber below,

Wails its dying pain

Tame the lion, I will

As the rose dies,

And the petals wilt

Anew rose has begun to live

The light will flourish
Once more
Gusts of wind dare to
Blow it out
A dying flame struggles for life

The numbers are passing,
Quite quickly now
It was once believed the end is
The only answer

The end can only
Be the beginning
From nothing,
Something emerges

Rain drop after rain drop
The flame lives

The Bad Man

Hush little devil
The bad man cannot see you,
If you do not look

Hush little devil,
The bad man cannot hear you,
If you do not speak

Hush little devil
The bad man cannot feel you,
If you hide beneath the covers

Hush little devil
The bad man is coming for you
The bad man will not find you if you keep still

Living Crumbs

A cake,
Decorated prettily with much frosting

Beneath a plain cake with a fiery filling
The sweet temptation sweeps over the hungry wolf

The wolf taking his time, consuming in delightful sneakiness
Alas, there lies another cake just a few feet away

A hungry wolf has to eat
Trailing behind him remnants of the expected cake

Only to be left as crumbs
To live in pieces of destruction

Cakes should not
Be eaten by wolves
That is life, just as a
mother bird will abandon
its flightless young

To Kiss

Such a small request
The desire so,
Is it truly the wanted item of
Discussion?

Between two so close,
Abandonment is feared most
Embraces are sacred

The ancients tell us of
How treasured the desire is
The most intimate of all
Things perhaps

The notion is not sexual
But loving
The meaning of a close bond
Breathe of life,
Touch them both so

Indeed the best was loved,
And so ever more

The Deceased Rose

Stumbling with each step
Torn anger

"Nevermore" mourn the
Weeping willows

Deep shadows pay
Their respects
Cold shoulders witness
The resurrection

The grass blade, stiff with hate
Dare not bend at each
Sorrowful prance

Unknown to the rest of the world,
Forgotten by many

Once the deed has been done,
Their lips sealed

A boney figure rises from
The burial plot
Moaning for help,
Groaning at the pain
Of late atonement

The end has barely began
Sweet deathly smells
Claim the air

The ghastly being holds out
Its hand,
"Like a kiss form a rose on a grave,"
To feel
Something real and alive
Horror-stricken, they run

Unsure of why,
It stands there alone
Not even the dead will accept it

The gown floats effortlessly
Around her fragile bones
She knows now that
She must go away

Atonement is not easy

To Write is to Paint

Coarse whispers outline

The image

The pen etches into the paper

The scar marks

Enclosed a picture

Few words spoken

Paint many images

A book of words

compares to

An oversized painting

A mural, if you will

Smeared Swirls

You are dripping again
Another rain storm
Is coming very soon

Believing you are worthless
Too much drama to handle
Every day

No "safe place" or that
Special "happy place" to disappear
Into for awhile
The sharp blade dances a fast hard
Rock beat over your body

Feeling so unalive
You can not think
Straight anymore

Everything has mixed,
Bleeding black streams of lies

You sit on the edge waiting for
The storm to pass
Have you ever known
A rain storm to last so long?
Dying today,

Crying for tomorrow
Will tomorrow ever come?

Begging for relief,
But no help comes

Life is many things,
And then you die

Far far away beckons
Your savior
"Hold on just awhile longer"
Whispers the wind

Your grip slowly loosens with
The passing of days

The time has come,
You must decide

Live for an unknown hopeful
Reason for someone
Or die in a miserable tragedy,
Alone and scared

The Piano Plays

Shushed notes are playing
In the ballroom
The pianist paints the picture as
It strokes the keys
One by one

Dream-like come alive the
Characters from long ago

Some dance,
Some run and play

Others simply watch in terror of
The beautiful scene illustrated

Blink and miss the best part
For once the mood has
Tired and over
The moment will be gone forever,
Until next time

Sweetly and tragically,
The notes ring
In the mourners' ears

As the music plays,
The truth begins to unfold

No one is right,
No one is wrong

Sit and watch
This is the best part,

That is all

The show never ends,
As time will always intertwine

Long after tomorrow has died
Here lies eternity
And repetition

Take a seat wherever you like
Every seat is a pleaser

Haunting Beauty of a Melody

Her heart weeping
Her soul screaming silently
In its secret hell

The horror of it all
Never been loved

Languishing somewhere in the
Tortured silence
Voices shaken with hate

Beloved stars,
Uttering the words
Feeling the lie
Stinging the tears,

Laughing silent agony
Raging raw hollow terror float
Into silver dreams

Silver dreams fly me away,
Save my soul

Shadowy arrivals drag me to
Plunge down a black
Shaft of despair

This small moment,
Inside a rain of tears create a
Deathless consciousness in
Swallowed hell

The dead silence, a seductive
Whisper ringing the
Bells of memory
Cries of hopeless tears of the
Frightened little girl I used to be

Soldiering on, I become
Devoured alive by bones
From the dusty ancient
Skeletons of past
Committed crimes

Hooded Guitar

Blaring the sounds of hell
Dreaming of the past

With a few scratches of a pen,
A horror flick begins

Careful strokes of the
Crowded sounds,
Show a story from the end,
Then the tragic beginning of the
Decayed destructions
Etches itself
Nicely into the flat screen

A burdened lie existing so that
Tomorrow,
The burial rite will not be done
To read

Gasping to exist, last held breathe
Slowly creeps out for just a peek

Sweet raptured light unguarded
By the splitted strings

Willed away pain
Comes back for more

The pain lives on,
Though the body is dead

Love Me a Little

Throw my soul in the trashcan
Stab my eyes

Flush the tears down the toilet
Runaway with your fears

Eat my heart
Torture my mind

Bleed some
Sew my lips shut

Bite the words I speak
Hang my love for you
On the gallows

Wildly blowing wind
Shoots through me

Your hand is too far to reach

The Cemetery is Closed

Molded tombstones
Faded engravings

Dead day old flowers
Lost graves

Consumed coffins
Dust bones lying restless

Six feet tall grass
Rusty gates
With all this death in the air,
Little grows here

No more visitors come
Everyone has paid their respects

The gravedigger, dead lying
Right over there
Under the burned decaying tree

No moonlight shines
over here anymore
Just another forgotten graveyard
Left to die

Hello Hangover Mornings

Deep deep down, blue is hot
And red is cold

Opposites are evens, therefore
Opposites do not attract
Likes do not repel but contract

Tip toe tip toe we go through
The strawberry meadow

Tick tock tick tock
What to do now

Run little child run as far as
You can go

If blue is hot then how is murder
Considered to be conducted by a
Cold blooded murder

Blood is blue, warm in the body
As so

Until oxidized, as it cools
Becomes red which is cold

Wet nails stroke the keys
Tap, tap
Click, click

Ring ring then
The answer machine

Liar Untold Lies

Mirror oh mirror on the wall
Mirrors do not lie, people do

Bang bang, a shot fired and
Somebody has died
Guns do not kill, people do

Snap snap, smile for the camera
A magical flash captures on a shiny
Thin film an image,
A photograph says
A million lies and stories

People do not know
How to not lie
A lying killer on the run with a box
Saying click, click
With every step

The Serenade

A few notes played

Tears stream down
Reminiscing over unknown memories
Dying for the hurt

All the pain thrives so hungrily
Unsure of why my eyes bleed of black lines
Whenever someone plays a few notes

No words need to be spoken
To be touched so much
By just a few notes

The Blue Lagoon

Gentle fingers glide across
Soft notes
Glasses spilling with shots of
Sweet sorrow

Deep-saddened souls falling into
The arms of their winged-demons

There goes another following his
Foot prints down the stairs

Blue music gracefully playing
He sits, drinking away to forget

With each sip, another sad note
screams out beautifully
The torment
Deep-saddened souls
Singing their pain

Listening to ruined old songs,

Watching them,

Seeing their future

He tells them the bitterness of

Truth, sparing their tiny hopes

"Sugar, we're all gonna die, you just
don't know when."

Live for now

Coconut Blue

Curled up by the fireside made
Upon the cement bed
Starry nights of no glory

Silver moon peeks and says boo

Today has gone
And long been over
Hello hello I say to yesterday
That replays again

Chipped nail polish shows the
Essence of life
Chopping down trees makes for
The early graves

Tick tock tick tock

Petals are falling down as the glass
Tips over spilling
All the water
Till there is but ice cubes in an
Empty glass

Words are but words my darling
Spoken then died
From exhaustion

The fireside porch lits up again
Bright red ashes fade
Into the bare air of nothing

Broken toys without
Mr. Gheppetto insight

Amy Oh Amy

Sweet intriguing innocence
Bare skin in view
Rumblings thoughts

Truth be shown,
You are who you are

The young and dear know the
Truth before the magical
Age of 7

Obstacles of tempting passions,
One rings as so and no more

A secret known to the keeper,
A secret for a new life

The flesh has rotten, a new sprout
Thrives from the chaos
Pretty little darling,
Confirmed the truth
Of the secret

A dream girl from the
Childhood lies,
A dream girl today

Dying Slowly

Dusty petals are raining down,
Prickling all that it touches

A wreathe of thorns
Clasp my wrists
Spiky chains tie
My ankles together
A frayed rope wraps
Around my scarred neck

Razors slice me all
Over my body
The dripping blood forms many
Puddles where I am sitting
Empty tears no longer
Stream down
These old worn-out clothes,
Tearing in the wind
A choir of angels stand in front
Of me, watching me die
Mercy painted on their faces,
Singing their forgiveness
The light has burnt out

The wall behind me has been

Lit on fire

Frustrated with hate, unsure of

What is happening

My guardian angel outstretches Its
pure innocent hand,

Wanting to take me home

But the nemesis of my heart

Begs me to come with

To the barbeque down

Under the iron gates

Been sitting her for

10,000 years, unable to chose

The one decision

I can not seem to make

Damn if I do, damn if I do not

Inside

Dead cold
Burning hate

Bleeding pain
A numbed heart

River of tears
Shattered feelings

Living for fear
Time dripping slowly

Misunderstood emotions
Tomorrow never comes

Sunlight tears
Through the darkness
A pain inside never dies

Sanctuary

Deliver me from quiet black lies
Whisper the distant
Sound of hope
Save me from myself

My heroes have long ago Crashed and burned
The burial rite,
Blank like the heavens
Fighting hell just to get here

Slowly fading, panting on
Your staircase
So weak that I can barely scream
Come, open the rusty gates,
Let me in

I am in need of
Some glowing guidance
This path is leading
To the streets
Give me a detour to heaven
Singing for my much
Sinned soul

Father help me,
I claim sanctuary
Please father, help me

The Hulk Within

You walked into this
Glass cage of horror
Gallows draw deep shadows
On the floor

Shrieks come from every corner
Gentle footsteps graciously dance
From behind the creaking walls

The sweet despair of nectar drools
From the corners of your
Dark empty black holes
Fighting a war with
Yourself from inside

Your thoughts inside your head,
Shoot out bullets
That pierce the hearts of
Unexpected souls

Your state of mind
Of being okay
Falls down as your soul crashes
Into the deck of cards

Each faceless card,
Has painted on another
Story of your hopeless life

All those years, flashing by
Someone is taking your picture
As you open
The locked wooden door,
A thousand years old,
Letting loose spirits of the dead
Changing your appearance

The past stays the same,
It is trying to throw you into
Your old trunk of yesterday
Only to let you out
For more torment

And your future morphs into
Something of a different
Walk of life

What will happen, will happen
No matter how much
You change

Black Clouds

My world trickles in dark blue flames
Down the broken mirror
Hanging like an accused
Innocent victim

I can feel my soul slide back into the
Chamber of yesterday

Echoing in the halls of hell, the
Death cry screams wrap
Around my neck loosely
But ready to choke me at any
Given moment

I cannot make it out myself
Lost the red flame on that black
Stick, trying to find myself

Chewing, tearing
This world is eating me alive
Leaving me here in the fog

Swollen red eyes
Blue tears dripping
Creating a river of tears

You are drifting away on soft
Thorns into the blazing sunset
That tears open the black screen
Filling it once again with light
To illuminate all the
Tiny light bulbs

Unaware

Death becomes her as she dies
Another day
As she stumbles toward the end of
Only the beginning
Of something alive
But long ago lived

Below the waters rage hungrily
Waiting so patiently once more
Too far from the rope to reach
Getting closer to the edge

As she thinks empty thoughts
Hoping and wishing, thinking
She will go somewhere nice

What a classic tragic ending
It will be
Does not know
What is happening

Fighting what she does not
Want to see
Drowning in the torrent
Sea of her demons

Overpowering her,
Pushing her closer
Lost in a daze of her
Own confusion
Surrounded by so much inside

Trapped, locked tight inside
Begging for relief

Oh savior,
Savior where art thou?

In Between Somewhere

Alone in a crowd
Scared in the light
Happy in the dark

Sane in the twilight
Insane in the emptiness

Lost in the sunshine
Found in the rain

Together in the fog
Loved in the wind
Hated in the moonlight

Shadowed in the sunset rays
Stuck, like gum on the bottom of your shoes,
In between worlds, lives, dimensions and dreams

Stalked by death
Abandoned by love

Cared for by fear and hate
Unwanted by life

Roses

Wilting in treacherous
Hurried beams of light
Meshed together
Dripping into a puddle of
Unspoken tortures

Time, flashing its camera
The ground, littered with pieces
Of many scandals
Many thorns prickling many

It is raining destroyed hopes and
Dreams once more
As each petal falls
From another rose,
Another tragedy has
Caught on fire

No water left to calm
The fiery devastations
So many roses falling apart
Dying ever so slowly in such
Blue waters

Real heroes are mere figures of
Hopeless destroyed roses wrapped
Tightly in plastic,
Peering out from the window
In the coldness
At the damned souls of the
Glossy window pane

Nowhere to be Found

A sweet buzz of angered silence
I remain here,
Alone with my thoughts
What I feel, will never go away

Soft hushes come from my
Sadistic heart
The repulsion of my own
Antipathy haunts me
Seeking, my antidote
In lost places
All lost, all gone

My treasures no longer in my
Greedy possession
Strength, Will, Joy, Fear
They too, have left

Is everything gone?
Did I disappear from the world?
Or is the world hiding from me?

There is no more left to lose
I have already lost myself

My babe departed
A long while now,
Before we were lucky
Enough to meet

My fate, the destiny I am
To lead,
Has changed many paths in
This short existence
Of the world

Trusting no one
I only trust myself to engage in
Suicide one day
Before my decomposing carcass
Finds a new bed to lie in

Last Night

Last night was another
Rough night
Had too much to dream
Last night

Wanted to leave, and find you
But I did not know where to go

Stepped one step closer to the
Brim of the broken glass,
That is glued together to
Keep me alive
I do not know what to do anymore
So many directions to go

Have you walked out of my life
Again?

Runaway lies have built the
Stone walls I am caged within

Lack of belief of some higher
Being has left me in the dark
Punishing me, leaving me in this
Windowless darkened room

I am dying here in the gutter
But I need you to find me

Deceived me so many times
But I need you now

Breathe life into me
With that kiss
That makes me feel like I have
Just woken up from the best
Dream I ever had

Come find me
Save me from myself

Shadows of Lowly Lies

Lowly lies of a solemn dirge

Dare not to enter

A state of ennui

The loveliest that lies nay be a woman but a man,

Yea be the drunkard, whom his hometown has not casted him

Loving those whom love presented themselves

He is not to be blame of their

Sudden disappearances

The latter he loved, a childhood

Sweetheart,

Did not go before he

But he before her

How so? No one knows

But time itself

The former, she went with a supposively untimely dire end

With her last bloody breathe, Whom did she see last?

Nay the death upon her eyes, The life in her cannot be!

Is it so?

A shadow of a shadow can tell no more

Bitten

Damned to heaven
Chained against my will to hell
The train heading towards limbo
Drifts away

Closed eyes, still seeing
All the damage
Corrupted inside
This jail cell has shrunk
Over the years

No voices to scream
Words have lost their meaning
The eerie silence grows each day
Hands becoming fists of rage

No where to run to for Sanctuary

The bite of one lonely wolf
Taints my soul

My blood raw and hot,
Gushing like a magical
Display of fireworks

Lonely and cold
Sad but happy with grief

Impatiently hiding behind the
Shadows of yesterday

The sharp blade becomes
My friend
Mr. Sharpy makes me feel better

Letting the pain bleed away

Picturesque

Paint the words
Draw your thoughts
Capture the flying
Away innocence

Black out the hate
Outline the love
Show the beauty
You have envisioned

Let this colorful canvas,
Look within its frame some of
The indescribable beauty
You foresee

In the creature, encaged upon
The portrait
Contains merely
An ounce of the glory

Inseminated Minds

From that gory bloodshed day
Blended by al the evil flowing,
Rushing to see you,
To taint you if it dare

Pure,
Oh so pure you are

Little darling be tempted not to
The hand that feeds
Be careful when walking in the
Light of day
At night you can hide
But not for long

It will not be long before you
Learn to crawl
Be quick to walk
And even swifter to run
Once you start running
Do not ever stop

The bad man is coming
After you

Wherever you go,
He will find you

A dozen years pass
Taught to be the
Intelligent animal
Though your actions are civil,
Your words refer to ancient acts
Of primal destruction

Now what,
Waste time to earn numerous
Pieces of paper

Living in hell just to get by
Not too far behind on the
Animal lifestyle

Dancing to Forget

The man with the heavily
Burdened soul,
Creeps out of the shadows
He is dancing again
In those ancient steps
Of such sacredness

As I walk slowly by
With so much interest,
He stops and nod
I too, nod

At the flap of the
Black crow's wing
Finding myself and the man in a
Wide-open meadow lighted by
The mere moonlight

All night he teaches
His unique dance
Together we dance to forget
Until dawn

The crow flaps its wings again
And perches itself upon
The man's sulked shoulders

Back in the empty streets with
So many yellow-filled sidewalks

Just as I turn to leave
Tears flow in rivers from his
Sleepless eyes,
Much sadness darkens
His features

Another man in the
Dark worn-out leather dusters
Stumbling with
Shots of memories

He also shows me
His unique dance
His dance told a story of death,
Torment and so many loses

Tomorrow night
I will show him my dance
A story of sadness, thorny
Betrayals and the persistence
To survive

Tinsel World

Everyone, alone forever
Lonely together
Seeking for the salty salvation

No hope left to go around
Screwing the system,

Dealing with a world of hurt
Becoming stronger
But still weak

Limiting everything
Dying slower than time
Begging for forgiveness

Receiving the torturous truth
Rejecting hateful benefits
From others

This world of ours
So perfect, so complete

Dreams of lollipops and
Ice cream sundaes
House made of ginger and spice

Innocence scents the air

Every day is perfection
It will not last

In Need Of

Oh pen in my hand
Write some words
Dig deeper into the
Dry well of imagination

Oh starry eyes
Look, what do you see
Lolly pop sticks with people's heads
on them?
Or razor blades falling
From the sky?

Mind's eye, what dwells in
My head
What story has not been told?

Come together
My precious ones
Help me be me again

Speechless
Thoughtless
Mindless

Dearest one draw me
Some inspiration

Make Me Believe

There is hope
The world is good

Lies and evil are mere fairytales
The truth is known

Pain is not pain
There is no such thing
As the bad man

Ecstasy is love
Drugs do not corrupt
Lies do not hurt

The living never die
Hope does not exist, it has
No need to be worshipped

Everything is okay
Nightmares are lies
Dreams always come true

All religions are one
And the same
Hate thrives only
In the shadows

Hell is not the bad place, just
Another world
The dead do not reign
Over the cemeteries

Love is pure and true
The world is not innocent

There is no such thing
As growing up
No one gets old
This world is Neverland

Understanding Them

To understand a monster

We must risk our survival in order to
look into their minds

From the cold hard squeaky seats
that sit there so patiently

In front of the black screen

Only then do we run the risk of

Letting them into our minds

And of course that is the

Moment when we truly

Understand the monsters

Realizing they are not

The monsters,

We are

Judging and classifying them

As a monster

Only because we cannot explain

Such inhumane acts of insanity

Truth inflicts much hurt and
Destruction onto others
But do we not act just like them
In our own simplistic ways?

We are the monsters
Of our nightmares,
That haunt us so viligently, only
Because we allow them to

For the same reason we know
Our kind cannot be stopped

For we truly are the monsters,
The only real monsters

Child of Mine

Hush little baby,
Do not say a word
The bad man is coming
To get you

If you should wake
Before you awake
Pray the angel of music
Keep your soul

Do not be fooled of the fallen
They have traveled the world
To find you

The cradle has fallen,
And so have you

Hush little baby,
Do not say a word
The bad man will not find you, If you keep quiet

Gruesome Montage

When the battle is over
Where do we go?

Why must the path
Be so unclear,
When we know home is near

The whispering truth
Chills our bones
Where are we going?
Will this pain lead us to where
We need to go?
Who have we become?

All the unsuspecting people,
Their lives continue
But ours have been changed far
Too much
Protecting the "innocent" from
Evil destruction

Our saviors gone with
The days of summer
They smile from up above,
In such a cruel manner

It is very brutal out there,
Many bloody revelations
Countless unwalked
Through bloody alleys

Thankless unknown, never seen,
Soon forgotten
They are fighting to live
As we fight for more luxuries
We cannot afford

Your Life

Singing the same ol' song
Writing the same ol' words
Living the same ol' lie

Pretending everyday to be
Someone else
Whose shoes have you been
Walking so many mile in?
You do not even recognize the
Face staring back at you,
When you gaze into the mirror

This is your world,
I am just passing through

A train speeding by, in the
Darkness of a lonely tunnel
Carved into a hundred year old
Mountain

I will not stay
This is not my boat to steer
Through the many windy rain
Storms of the deep sea
I am here now, but not for long

A bummer sticker fading away,
Piece by piece, slowly tearing off
The glassy surface
Eat your dinner
Before it gets cold

The Alternate Way of Life

Hope
Sanctuary
Comfort in the darkness

A home for now
A home forever more

Understanding minds
Similar thoughts
Dead inside
But the heart beats faintly

Tears of black line the eye
As blood covers the lips

Sweet tainted seraphs
Gentle demonic creatures
A devil of every kind
All come together
No judgment

Dark customs
Traditional words

A rainbow of your choice
Long, spiked
Or short and messy

Ink decorates the body
Of what lies in the soul

Additional holes let out the pain
Beautifully alive
Yet dead in spirit

The Daily Nightmare

The walls shook,
The mirror fell

Still the pieces remained
Looked out the frame opening
Saw blood stains
Piles of salt in every corner

I mimed the creature's action
It screamed
And the pieces came apart

A somber silence fell over us
The sight alive only in the pieces

No remembrance
For the wicked

Say Cheese

Stolen memories captured
Framed on white walls
Kept in books
With many captions
Every turned page, a new story

Fun happy clips remembered
Sad angry threads forgotten
CD cases line the bookshelves

Many moments stolen kept on
Slices of plastic and wood
Pieces of souls marked and
Tagged namelessly with color

The pictures reflect
On the mirror
Show what was truly felt at that
Moment in time
Encased forever
Trapped in the feeling forever

Prisoner in time
Scribbled letters on the black,
The white smooth surface
Depict the time
And date it was taken
Never what happened before or
After the flash

Here comes the camera men
All dressed in mysterious horror

In the tiny hole, I see you
Smile, click, flash
Dancing stars, goodbye

Petals

Rose flesh

Leaves of autumn

Glowing orbs

Sparkling dimples

Ruby red jewels of delight

The little brown house,

So delicate

Yet so strong against

Gusty winds

Smoke clouds of love floats from the dusty chimney

Well-tended roses bloom brightly of the gloomy days

In the front yard

A quiet stream flows in a beautiful waterfall,

Surrounded by the rose

Not old, just older

A Rainbow for You

In my hands I bear a secret
The truth will be told
All will be done as it was written
A long long time ago
Home is what you make of it

I kneel before you
Here take it

Never lose sight of it
This tiny treasure is worth
More than gold itself
This is yours to keep,
No one else's to touch
Keep it secret, keep it safe

I present to you
Something magnificent
Not many have one
But yours is big enough for two

Do not look, close your eyes
And open your hands
Take it now, run
Run far, far away

When you have stopped
Running and have tired,
Remember what I gave you

It is not one a kind but it was
Made just for you and the other

When the special other is found,
Share the treasured keepsake
Reassure the other it is yours
And both to keep

Now go
Run, run as far as you can run

Your soul is your guide
Believe in your heart
Trust in your heart

Drifting in a Wooden Crate

Swoosh, back and forth
The sound,
Only the ocean can make
Stinging ribbons brightly
Stab thy eyes

A croaky moan whispers
Shhh, the waves seem to say

Flittering clams barely open,
The images everywhere
And meshed together
Is it a face from heaven
Or the devil by your side

Mmmm, the taste of fear
And enchantment
With a cup of confusion
And dash of wonder

Land nor sea,
Sky nor ground

Is this heaven or hell?
Or the doorway home
To the lost world?

Wherever you go,
Lost and lonely
Still you will remain

The Poet

A writer of heart
Each stroke bearing
The skins of souls

Rhyming to love,
While watching a dove die

A romantic by mind
But forgot to let loose

Unable to trust
In words, keeping the peace
Between the world

Living alone and
So lonely for love
Paper full of words,
Entangling within it
The true feelings

Swept under the carpet,
Promises of finding the one

Each poem, she lives in a dream
She forgets the past
And remembers the better times

One day, love will find
Its way home to her
'Til that day,
Her poetry is her romance

The Path of Death

The artist, dark of mood,
Bright soft complexion
The soul, scarred

A bleeding heart lies in the
Hands of a demon
Series of pictures flash
In the decaying mind

Only words can show
What lies inside
The sketches badly drawn,
Weak in detail
Merely windows

Thy words speak to thee,
The artist to the demon
Upon the door
To what is kept inside,
Angry words paint it

Thy sweet demon, weepeth not

"Nevermore," beckons from
Upon the shoulders

Of the phantom
Who lingers in the shadows,
Awaiting the artist

Deep inhumane roars
Scream out from thee

Heaven leaks of blood,
Below home sweet home rumbles

Hello, Sweet Child

Sugar-coated regrets
Bitter-sweet memories

Long lost feelings
Blinded, seeing what you
Never took the time to see
Alone but not lonely

Reminiscing
Fingers gliding over glossy
Pictures of what use to be
Each turned page,
Every new picture sparkling
Clips from the movie
Of your life

Gentle fingers dancing across
Antiques of the past
Eyes smiling with
Intrigue and curiosity
Patient ears listening carefully
Clinging to your every word
Of worn-out stories

Sometimes even rags and scraps
Can make beautiful things
Walls covered in frames,
Preserving the young

A young hand clasping
An old hand as they both
Wander down Memory Lane,
Once again

Writer's Block

The words have run dry

Thoughts and dreams,
Blank with emotion
Imagination tired
And overworked

Inspiration gone into the world,
Back where it belongs

Patience is still
The pen, eager to write
But the mind unsure of
What to say

A whirlwind inside
Stop the madness
Stop time for 5 minutes

Breathing is not the same anymore
Many fear this disease
Curable but time consuming

New light is needed to see
Beauty lies in all things

The poet,
Unable to share the beauty seen

Too many words running wildly
All trying to be written at once
Imagination has lost its savior

Come back the pen screams
To write is to live

Poetry, children's stories
For the adults
Truth, lies, sex, multiple worlds
All part of what makes
A great poem

Draw me a picture
Give me some inspiration

Just Live

Let your heart run wild

Never know until

You take a chance

Chase your dreams

Hold on to your hopes

Let go of all your

Balloon bunches of fear

Live again

Life

Burned by love
Scarred by hate

Yet I still can walk
Among the living, alive
Full of fear with
Danger stalking me

Splintered by hope
Cut by dreams
Shadowed by wisdom
Comforted by fear

Betrayed by love
Entrusted by fear

Corrupted by society
Broken by life
Drowned by lies

Suffocated by the truth
Blinded by freedom
Engulfed by justice

Consumed by everything
Condemned by the media

Redemption

Facing the music

Looking into the courtroom

Listening to the truth

Feeling once again

The pain of lies

Remembering the past

Dealing with the memories

The pictures of long ago

Lived moments,

Plastered to the walls

Of your mind

Hating yourself for

Mistaken choices

Trying to forget what you did

And all the wronged you caused

Atoning for your past

Trying to fix the present

Changing, creating the future

Your life recreated once again

Accepting poor misfortunes, Until tomorrow

Paradise Hell Lifestyle

Trying to survive

In a world so cold

Surviving with no justice

Fighting to live

Battling hell at night

Manipulating others

In the day, living in paradise

Buying some time with blood

Never go alone

Always armed

Constantly ready

Sound familiar?

Life Goes On

Unknown fear
Everlasting hate

Short-lived love
No trust

Infinite choices
Suffocating lies

Stabbing truth
Unrecognizable feelings

Dazed in wonder,
Soaking in the sunshine
Million-pieced puzzles
Of confusion

Highways of darkness
Leading to everywhere

Ships of bright light in churning
Crystal green waters
Of a fiery storm

Bulldozed pain and agony upon the steaming hot pavement

Shattered lives

It ends here at the cross roads

Goodbye is forever,

Hello is now and sometime later

Towns painted in lies

Awaiting anticipation

Begging for loneliness

Disregarding everyone else

Wanting what you have,

Needing nothing

Silence Is Golden

Silence is murderous
Silence is deadly
Silence is a serial killer

Silence is a monster
Silence is everything
Silence is fear

Silence is hate
Silence is love
Silence is nothing at all

Silence is never ends
Silence is silent

Silence creeps in every corner,
It is everywhere
Silence consumes
Their very being,
Leaving them behind as a pile of
Forgotten bones in a graveyard

They eat, breathe and sleep
With silence

Silent eyes tell of a world so
Cold and lonely yet noisy and
Of graveyard beds and tables

Silent ears wait anxiously
For safe silence,
They fear complete silence
Silence is an eerie soft gentle
Lullaby to silent ears

Silent lips speak in code-silence
Silent bodies shiver in the cold
Silence of explosions

Silent faces will
Never be the same

Silent soldiers have seen
Too much to be able
To live again,
As they once did

Silence is a bright star of hope
In the powdery-gray
Clouded sky

Silence...always on...
Never fading away

Silence forever more silence
Silence never dies

Forgotten soldiers
Forever more remain in
Complete silence

Shallow Graves

Gravedigger burying souls
Deep in the ground
Making every grave so shallow,
So they may all feel the rain

Their time has come
For them to remember
And let go

When the rain comes,
It washes everything away
All the tears gone
No more fears left to haunt

Rainy days, dreary eyes
Sad faces bleeding their pain
Sore voices tired of screaming

Eyes, can drip endlessly with
Haunted house mirrors of the past,
Present And Future
Cut dreams, broken lives

Everything is mended here,
Piece by piece, every memory,
Every forgotten thought

The gravedigger becomes
The puzzler
Much like a bartender,
Knows you well,
All your memories, stories,
Everything you ever felt

Gravedigger,
Digging those shallow graves
Again

Another rainy day
Is coming soon

Kiss of Death

You have read my burial rite
And I am singing my sorrow

Were my actions so horrible?
You always were a hot head
But never did you hit me
Though your angry soft spoken
Words felt like blades
Cutting me deeper than
My own sharp suicidal tendencies

Oh and your actions,
Always giving me
The cold shoulder
Leaving me to wonder
If you were going
To commit suicide or not

When you met me, I saw
Something in your eyes
A small flame flickered
Blinded by your beauty and
Safety in your arms

Now I know all you are
Is a monster
A sad little boyish monster

Hmpf! And it was you who
Wished me to hell

But haha! Not before
I wished you death first

Oh how delightful, the way
We meant death upon
One another

One and the Same

Heaven so sweet and perfect
Such pleasant blissfulness

No more pain
Suffering will cease to live
A life in eternal happiness

What a beautiful mirage,
That is so hot and fiery
Camouflaged in
Pillow-soft clouds

The bright light, blindingly
Shining from deep within
The concealed pit of boiling hot
Hellfire at the center of life itself

The sweet lick of an ice cream
Scoop on a sugary cone,
Morphs into the bitter-alcohol
Worm at the bottom
Of the unopened Tequila bottle
Clasped in a
Drunken man's hand

It will never be the same
Such tainted pureness

A virgin of hate no longer
Seraphs singing softly of
Sweet sorrow for all
No more shall stained souls
Return to their sanctuary

The end has long been near
Heaven + Hell = Our world

Haven of Mine

Oblivion
Peering inside my world
I begin to feel at home
Safe from the world

The sun shines down
Candy clouds of cotton
Gumdrops fall like rain
From the sky

Fresh dewy grass tickles
My dirtied feet
Laughter overwhelms me

Fear and hate,
I know not while here
Books line the shelves that
Gate my world

Cartoon heroes, here and there
I am safe here
From my fears,
My enemies and myself

Run, play
Hide and seek, favorite game

The playground,
My favorite place to be
The slides so slippery
The swings, swinging so high
This sand, never soiled,
Never tainted

Bare foot, I run
Dancing to the music
In my head

Remain here
Housed comfortably
Inside my consciousness

Canvas Unrated

A picture is worth
A thousand words
What defines the emotion felt
From something 2-dimenisonal?

One strong emotion or many
Will be drawn from this picture
It is not obvious,
For feelings generally are not

The secret lies within,
Deep within
Another conquest
For the answer

No biases of any kind
Are allowed
The past shall remain where it
Stands, in the past
The present should <u>not</u> be
Taken into consideration
Nor the future

Simply the situation alone,
Can deem what will be
In the painting
Colors, objects, things

Whatever is needed
To find the answer
How long will it take
For the finished effect?
Time cannot tell
Perhaps the heart can,
If it dares to reopen

Where will this painting grow?
In mind or on paper?

Either or, one would presume
Both, maybe, to understand
The full effect

The thought,
The memory
Which is which?
Undetermined emotions
Mold themselves

Snap and You Are Awake

The years have gone of
Youth's bitter happiness
Nay can I forget the memories
What brings like, attempts to
Take it back

Through water in judgment
At midnight's hour, rest at last
Awoken not yet from
This dream
Still does fire rain down
And frozen lamps light the way

Poison on your hips,
What does it mean?
Left is the rebel way,
Is that why your gun smokes
On your left?

Air, oh air
You find it hard to catch it
Swallow the pills,
Maybe happiness
Will come back

Shhhh......
On the seventh day of tomorrow,
You will remember to breathe
Awakening in the arms
Of a seraph

As tomorrow nears,
Hope dies

All is lost

But not lost forever
For everything lost has its place,
Somewhere over the rainbow

A Word with the Undertaker

Body bags
Toe tags
Need a rag?

Do not breathe in too deep
What a perfect place to sleep
Six feet under the steep

Been in business since the
Weekend after the dawn of time
Sublime is it not
I feel like a mime whenever
I look in the mirror

Ghosts, they are such
Nice hosts to meet
Most will shake your hand
Do not boast or
They will rattle your bones

Death,
A breathe of life
With rotten teeth

Bones shaking
Moans and groans here
And there
Will you loan me your phone

Life cuts deep and sharp
Just like a knife

There is an open grave
Over there
Be brave and take a peek

This is the end now
So stay low to the ground

Because they will throw you
Into a coffin

Remember home is where
The tombstone lies

Teen Life

A lonely child lost in a crowd

Never knowing when

The day will come

Wanting to feel something real

Addicted to the pain,

Screeching inside

Rainfalls over the marbled stones gazing into oblivion

Wondering how it will all end

Sitting,

Slouched over,

Head lying so tiredly over bones from the past

Confusion strikes again

Fear, more powerful controls
The now mindless empty body
Whilst pricking itself
On a rose thorn
Much like a kiss from a rose
On a grave

Bed of ashes
Pillows of wood,
Blanketed with dirt,
The headstone lying there
So peacefully,
Mourning the dead

A New World In Pandora's Box

One world, many dimensions
Lies everywhere

Tall tales explaining the truth
Mishap of calculations
Can be disastrous
We seem to hang at the edge
Of destruction
Unsure of what to do next,
Or where to go from there

Committing shameful acts
Of deforming divinity
Such cruelty becoming
Part of daily life

Accepting our own destruction
As the "new normal world"
Making other creatures adapt to
Our "newly created world"

Mendling with the divine secrets
Of life itself

Technology, our compass,
Directing all into
The "new world" of our arrival
Jinxing our chances for
New possibilities of life
By unbalanced
Controlling thoughts

Creating catastrophic
Consequences for much of the
World's future and present

The past, merely arrangements
Of material to be newly formed
Into other mutated
Forms of material

Human society, another colorful
Strand in the quilt, the blanket
That binds all life together

Reminiscing over sweet
Promiseful lies of extinction

The need for more
communication is becoming
Dangerously critical
To the need of the whole
Human society

Little does anyone listen
With their ears,
So focused on the horror from
The screeches of the
Ignorant eye

More damage, less construction
To the devastations at hand
Continuously making time
To conquer other worlds

Trying to keep control of
Human society under one rule

Prevailment of a Holocaust

Numb devastation
Death is inevitable, so is life
Destiny remains
Not on one path

Blank quiet emotions
Craving horror of truth

Procuring allayment
Prudent gentiles line the
Overstocked moldy closet

Sundry execrations
Comprised within the hell
Disdained convalescent creatures

They walk together,
They die together

Tricked to think this would
Be a dream

In they go,

One by one

Smell that, it is them rotting

And burning

In, naked with shame

Out, cold and dead

Beautiful lies color their disdain

And fragile morale

Hip, hip hurray!!

Today you might die

Oh excuse me,

Go ahead, you first

We are all last in the end

Ta ta for now!

Stains in Time

We leave our lives
In such tainted echoes

Hoping there is something
Pleasant waiting for
Our damned souls

Ruined our pureness
With our curiosities
Young lies die hard

We are all breaking down
In limited time

Death shuffles
Our untimely fates
In a game of poker
With the devil

In traceable fears for tomorrow
We have blue hopes and
Grim emotions for life

Surprises store
Around every corner
Making mere happiness
Another hopeless dream
Slipping, falling into the hand of
Our own destruction

Facing death each day,
Living lazily with broken hearts

Images mocking us
From their glassy surfaces

Bulldozing over our own graves
Creating but destroying
Wondering with such
Enthusthiastic curiosity

Searching beyond,
Forgetting the way home
Begging for peace

The same peace we ruined with
Our many successful
And useless inventions

Quitting, struggling through the
Swamp of our past

Murdering ourselves from with
Killing the world softly
Finding solitude never again

Welcome home everyone,
We are all here to stay

Fallen Star

Innocent by lack of experience
Finding comfort in the arms
Of darkness

The imagination so creative
Almost childish

Clouded thoughts rambling
Dancing sadistically through the
Smashing shattered pieces,
Is the cold the bite of blood

Poetically they run to fit
Themselves back,
To as they should be
A whole, not a puzzle

Your essence here
Fills the emptiness
But when you are gone,
I am alone again

My broken heart needs your so
Leave me and I will die

The Man Who Speaks French

His stature,
Tall and sophisticated
The intelligence, the same
As any other human

His mind, old in thoughts
Yet young in age
Glasses or contacts,
Handsome still

I tell my every secret
For I know I will never be
Judged in his eyes

His singing voice,
A fatherly lullaby in
Little French words

Dare he not curse in English
But in French everything goes
For many know not
His secretive language

He wants to run for senate,
He will I know
Someday soon,
He will be in public office
And I will be there in the
Outskirts of the crowd,
Cheering him on

He is a good man,
With a magnificent heart

Roman customs
But French spoken words

One day soon,
He will be President
And I will be the first
To toilet paper his house

Impossible you say ha!
I will prove you wrong!

Anything is possible,
Given enough persistence

Miles Away

Looking in
Perceiving what is there
Speechless to the
Dimension ahead

Hiding again
You are not safe here
Or anywhere else

Living for a few moments
Each time
With every look you catch peering in
Wondering what everything is

Touching the glassy plate,
Feeling something
It has been too long since
You have felt what pain was

Wishing you could feel
What they are feeling
No matter how much
It would hurt

When will you find you way
The path is just
Over the horizon

But you are busy, digging
Time to lie in the grave
You have dug

Maybe a Doorway Home

My window is open
I think I will jump
And take a plunge
To my premature burial

Seems like such a gloomy day
To die
It is a perfectly gruesome day
For an endless vacation

The opened caged door,
Shows of the vast plains and
Blocks of hell

Damned heaven I lie,
Soaking in on this bed
My wings beg to fly
The feathers sadly drift to the
Cherished ground

Tears of lustful sorrow
Bind my soul

Leave I can never go
Body and mind,
Lost and forgotten

The soul, dearly departed
On three, I will go
An evil number, yes indeed
One...two...three...

Not today, not today
Tomorrow today
Tomorrow tomorrow

Tomorrow I will be done
I will be home and fine at last

Still Dream

Begged for the moon
Asked the stars
To come and play
All that came was a fallen sky
Upon my tiresome shoulders,
Steadily I walk with the burdened sky

My every issue troubles me daily
Death lies lazily
Amongst my thoughts
At my age, death is all
I can think of

Such an utter disappointment
To the childish image of myself
Looser becomes the string,
Blown away are my
Hopes and dreams

I stand here, still and alone
No creature dares come
To my side

Not worthy of even the vilest
Of all creature's comfort
The burden I carry is mine alone
Others try to help
But I will not let them

It is now my duty
To keep the sky upright,
And in its place

Deliverance From Myself

I want to die, my body cries
Come with me, my soul bellows
From the sweet blissful
Heaven above

There are no words left to
Describe the hate
The hurt inside rises and
Falls like the raging ball of fire

Shaky nerves calm down as the
Thunderstorm lessens a little
Is there no God?
Something to worship to take
Away my sins

Have I not served my time?
This world I live in,
It is hell within itself

My wings have been clipped,
My heart decorates the floor
In shattered fragments
The mirror never lies

My mind goes to great limits to
Amuse itself with my sufferings

I see no body, perfect by nature,
The creature that I see is
My own reflection

Am I the monster
I stare at every morning?
What have I become?

And so I shall pass my crown of
Thorns onto you
No more blood bleeds
From my veins

Awakening in Lucifer's blessed arms,
I will have absolution

White Lace on Black Feathers

The crow cries for what it
Wanted and has lost
A sorrowed one mourns deeply
In the twilight of night

Captured the white lace
From the fallen hands of
Another's sweet heart

Tighter the lace wraps around
The crows feathered throat
Sweet mellowed sheet of black
Patches slowly floats away

The coming of the gentle wind
Encourages the crow to
Join in death

Alas the feathered being
Lets go of its last
Cherished breath

Just above the horizon,
The winged-demons march
Ever so graciously

Swiftly the red angel rises
From the depths of hell
But the red angel has come
Too late,
Gone way with its sins,
The crow is taken in the arms of
The winged-demons

The crow loved and lost,
Not only itself but the
Sweetheart of another

In the Corner Crying

Not so long ago,
I cried for the first time

The pain in my heart,
Was so great I had to bury it

As I sat there in the corner,
Contemplating death

For a moment,
I wished to be a slut
Getting my loving on the run

I tried to stand and run
So I could get laid
And feel what it feels like
To be loved

No matter if it was not true
I did not care,
I do not care now

Burned by teardrops of love
Drowning in this puddle of hate

Since the day, I first cried
The pain in my heart has
Only grown

Innocently touched
Too damn curious
For my own good

With my knees bent to my chest
And my head lying
Between my arms and knees
I cry in this stance,
Every time I hurt

I have loved and lost
Many times

My heart, a bucket of dust
And my soul,
Strung around my neck

All that remains innocent,
Lies in my crotch

I do not know who I am

My sadness has grown into a
Monstrous being,
The monster that hides
Under my bed

The bad man is after me
He hides in the shadows
Watching and waiting

Memories in a Garbage Can

Remembering is a curse
Forgetting becomes a talent
Reliving the moment in dreams

I do not want to
Reminisce anymore,
These memories, those thoughts
Are eating me whole
I have become consumed
By own destruction

Allow my heart to heal
As I drive into
My ocean of tears
Letting go of all my fears
Cannot bear this unending
Torment of hell

The walls are cracking
And falling down,
Brick by brick
I want to be someone
I once was and can no longer be

Let your essence
Float away from me
This is the last
You will hear from me

The lid is melted shut
I am the memory within
My memories of you and me
And a few others

Adult-Child

It began in the spring,
Late spring

Summer was running late
Friends laughed and rejoiced
A few unknown drunks died
And a couple of
Innocent bystanders

Nature, the number one killer
Love kills,
As one young mind discovered

The sadness is an
All consuming flame
Yea the years were short but
The pain lasts still

All loves gone
Alas but one

Once the four years have ended
A lifetime merely begins

An orange balloon
Tied to my throat
Months and now
A year has passed

A badge with my name on it
Poor as the poor homeless

Where does time go
Once you grow up?

Our Home Is Your Home

The pen bleeds of ink,
As my heart drains itself of tears

My body broken and blue
Eyes of the past
Intensify their glare
The lonely and lost
Dwell with me

Here, we remain
In a far far far away land
No deeds to be done

Many shattered mirrors
To pick up and dispose of
The beat, the sound,
The soul emotion

Words trapped in cages,
Hearts locked for keepsakes
The trunk becomes unbearably
Full of secrets

Curses born,
Truth told
Lies dead,
Dreams run wild here

This place it is a heavenly hell
A hellic heaven

This is home to those
Lost and broken

Cursed and fallen
Blessed and cheated
Abandon and hungry

This is home

On the Verge

On the verge of a breakdown
A real meltdown of the
Sticky matter

Incased in a box of
Shattered stone and colored glass
Sulky dreariness rains down
Fainter my voice becomes

I matter!
I will not be ignored anymore
The crowd begs for
The plunge of my death
Should I give them
What they want?

"Stay," a lonely voice whispers
From the seething mob
"Stay for what?!," I scream
But the voice never spoke again

Stayed I did,
For the hope of
Something better

I want to leave but that tiny
Shred of hope keeps me here
And the voice that spoke
So long ago

Stay I will until the hope
Crumbles away into nothing

Faceless

Molest this body
Lay thy head on the surface
Feel the warmth radiate
From the skin
Hear the thump
Of the precious heart

Steal a glance from
Those glossy sockets
Stare and see the monster created from within

Cut with careful ease, tiny marks dance all over the corpse
Gently caress, running your scarred hands through
The dingy oily hair

Savor every second
Remember the moment

Feel the soft plushes of decaying skin from beneath scarred
Rough bleeding fingers

This body, this moment,
The overwhelming sensation of Ecstasy

All seems so untrue
Deceitful those eyes are

That mouth,
Bleeding from the corners Becomes ever so tempting

Just a taste will do
A simple, small little bite

A Blue Rose

Lived a wonderful life,
The future held a tragic ending

Stabbed by love
Aching for him

The world sends friendly
Reminders of him each day
Yet everyone seems to be
Against two of a kind

The boulder wanted time to
Accept them
But the rose defied him

She could not bear
Not being with the one
Somehow the boulder
Understood but is
Too stubborn to accept

A lifetime of sorrow led to
Eternal happiness
So many times they try
To be together
But fate takes another route

Destined to be together
The world against them,
Having big plans
For the two of a kind

Piles of papers and some
Notebooks capture her pain
She writes to save the memories
Pictures were not meant
For the sad
But a pen and paper are

Remember To Breathe

Breathe in
The daily horror is just
About to begin
Are you ready?

Wait, put on a little make-up
No one needs to see the scars
Do not forget the mascara
And eye shadow
Oh and put on your best shoes

There is no reason
You cannot look pretty
Even if you are having a bad day
Ahem, excuse me
I mean shitty life

Oh sweetie it is okay,
Do not cry
Here, dab those beautiful eyes

Put a smile on,
You are already wearing
Your happy mask
Accessorize!

Come here,
Put your hand in mine

No matter what happens today,
Remember to breathe
Relax and breathe okay

You will do great
Keep your head up
Flash that gorgeous smile

And do not forget to breathe
Now breathe out

Atonement

The truth is known
Secrets told
Lies smeared across my face
I look for forgiveness
Atone my soul,

First strike forgiven
And forgotten
Second strike simply stupid

You tested me and I failed
I tried harder but fell
From the cross

Here I walk
Naked and cold
Bare-footed and mindless

Oh savior, where are you
Guardian angel help me
There will be no third strike
I am sure of it

I question your demands
I pushed you

Now I am here to get you back
Will you take my hand?
Where are you now?

Do not let me die here
Love is a
Never-ending forgiveness
So why have you turned
Your heart on me?

Misleading hurts so much
Is that what you
Wanted me to feel?

I am dying without you
Your monsterish being has
Forbidden you from me

I guess you do not believe in
Second chances,
As I did with you

Hermaphadite Dolls

She saw a pretty penis
One summer morning

In her imagination,
She has both sexes
One sex is simply
A disfigurement on evolution
A disgusting mutation

Flowers and clams are perfect
With two of a kind
So why cannot she

Beautiful soul
How about a beautiful body
Who deems it not so?
One day soon,
She will be perfect
In body and mind

Thoughtful he is
The same he wishes to be
But more of the opposite sex
Than both

Lesbians perhaps,
If the change was made for him
As for her, she can hardly wait
To have a penis of her own
The ability to pee anywhere
A pretty penis it will be
Strap-ons are just silly
The truer she is, the better

Off they will go to
The Wonderful Wizard of Oz
She will get her pretty penis
And he will become a woman
Or merely a man with boobies

Oh fun it will be
Two hermaphadites perhaps
Or maybe one and a half

Friends forever more
Through every sex change
Of perfection
At last they will be perfect
In one another's eyes
And one day in their lover's eyes

Oh joy, they both can hardly
Await that beautiful day

Beloved Passerby

Bite my lip
As I bite my thumb to you
Tear my soul while I peel
Away the layers of your life
Eat my heart as I make the
Extra effort to break yours

Capture the sunlight
Of my happiness,
I will be yours to keep

Thread a needle through these
Soulless sockets
Kill me now in my sleep,
So that I feel no pain

These emotions are tingling
The sensation is
Unusual and odd

Strange may be your customs,
But still I will obey

Bring me a cup of water
And I will spit it back
In your mouth

Make me yours to keep

The animalistic instincts beg to
Come and play
Let my tendencies
Run wild and free,
Like the spurting foundation of
My gushing blood

Cut me and bleed
I will for your enjoyment
The joints that hold my bones
Together ache in all the walking
I have done
Going to hell and back

My purse is full of the ashes
From the past
My body keeps the scars close
To it that come from my history

Habits of past lived days
Haunt me and now you
This corpse I occupy is rotting
Rather quickly from
The inside out

Splash my eyes with the oils
From the painted portrait
That you live,
So that I may see what you see
Show me your beliefs

Let me live your nightmares
Own my life or give it back

I am done dying
Life has no want with me
Death has abandoned me

I am simply a passerby
Here to stay,
If allowed by your graciousness

These shoulders
Burdened by love
And destroyed by the truth

Your uttered words
Bring me pleasure
I laugh at your pain
You fall to the ground bawling
When I smile

Bite your tongue
I will not speak at you level

You are lower than me
I own your life yet you have
Held me prisoned

At the simple utter
Of your breathe,
I could have your throat
But you intrigue me

Your disgusting being oddly
Interests me intensely
Your slimy soul brightly lit
As a shiny rosebud

I find you gross and icky
Yet I speak to you
As if we were equal
But you are below me

I socialize with you like another
Commoner of my stature

Why do I do this?
Who are you?

Set me free,
I am not yours to keep

The Television Set

The box with moving pictures,
The pictures laugh and scream
Frolicking in the death of
So many emotions
Their humor in the
Tragedy of happiness

Plastic buttons
Change the scenery
Educational thrillers roam
Across the hot glass

The noisy box
Moans and groans
Prolonged use causes it many
Aches and pains

The subliminal messages
Become the truths in life
The daily ritual of
Babysitting a box with
Moving pictures
How intriguing!

What a lovely way to
Spend one's time!
As the mind rots,
The body quickly becomes
Bloated and quite large

A meal is not the same without
Thy faithful companion
Always there, sitting on a table
The electric bill surprisingly
Rises each month
Little by little

Need a light?
Turn on the set
What could be a
Better night light?

Unisex Heart

Live today, love someone,
And lose something hidden
Live in tragedy,
Earn your soul mate's love
In the end

A special flower,
Exotic with your thoughts
But still not fulfilled

The dog continues to growl and
Pull on your black shirt
"Shhh…, go away"

Louder and louder
It barks each day
"Shhh.… Shut up or I will put you
away forever"
Your ravenous dog
Whimpers and quiets

In the treasure chest,
Lies a secret

Roses pass but they never really
See the beauty in others

Only their pain and tragedy

Oh sweet flower,
Why do you weep so
Come tell me willow tree,
What is wrong

I am sure the tiger
Will understand
He tends to your daily needs
In return you bring him,
Beauty and love daily

What to do
So many choices, so confused
Your mind says you love him
Your heart says
He is your only one

But your body craves both
Flowers and lions
Which do you choose?

True you are to him and always
Yet you feel unfaithful for
Your wandering mind
His wanders but not
As far as yours
Or does it?

He partly knows the truth
Will he remain yours?

Your innocence has been
Left behind
Redeem your soul

Be honest to him
For he never lies to you

"Oh but he does"

Admit to him
Admit to yourself

Ballroom Enchantment

Ah Claudette,
Your thin beauty so magnificent

Dear Edward take mine hand,
Dance with me my darling

How sweet you are rue
Has your phantom arrived also?

Three unisex hearts,
One lovely rose
Forever vines entwined

Dear Edward, come
May I take you on a walk into a
World you have not seen until Now?

Ah Claudette,
Pretty dirty little mistress
Have you not found a lover to Keep?

Oh sweet rue
You roam the town,
Nowhere is your demon fairy
To be found
Oh where,
Oh where could he be?

Dear Edward, dance with me

Ah Claudette, I see you found a
Stranger to play with
Careful now,
All roses prick

Claudette, I see you

I know you have been hiding
I have come to play
Will you not play with me
For awhile?

Come, let us take a walk
Tell me where you want to go,
I can take you anywhere

Beautiful you are, nonetheless
Imperfections, where?!
If no other dares not love you,
I will

Remember to breathe
If all else shall fail,
Breathe and remember
I love you

Let us go rose picking
In the garden
The deader, the better

Smile, I know you want to
Do not mind Edward,
He will not take me from you
I will not let him

Claudette, I see you
You look lovelier each day

My dearest and prettiest friend,
I love you

Inhalation

Ghastly breathing

Stomach churning

Of many sweets

Strong urges to puke carcasses of ashes from the once living

Lips cracking, very much dry

Laced with small white and black particles

Seems to snow shredded pieces of old colorless movies

The burnt aroma,

More stench of death

Fixated thoughts

Etched into gleaming plates

With sweat, reeking concentration and hope

Mourners laughing,

Tolling their deathly bells

A thin blanket envelopes

Our souls,

Letting us choke on our own Premonitions

Smoke fires of hell will engulf us All soon

Dare we give into temptation?

Seeing All With A Glance

Quiet meadows hiding deep
Burdened secrets

Such tamed stillness

Among the rows and columns

Of carved marble,

Resting and rotting,

The remnants of days that

Lived and died

Small sacrificial offerings decorate

Some of the sheets of carved marble

Gentle breezes kissing the leaves

With great softness

Fluttering wings in the rain

Peacefulness,

The view from the gates

The screen of this

Beautiful garden is so deceitful

Petals fall down for hope of

Tomorrow's arrival

Dugged holes leave the pathway

As spotted a snow leopard

The clouds, playing
Amongst themselves games
Thundering their anger
With each shot
Gusty winds are here to stay

Sunlight tickles many
Worn-out branches
A breathe of sigh squeaks
Through the rusty gates

Rotting fruit paints
The high walls
Protecting the disturbed garden
From its common self that begs
Anxiously to be let out
Into the garden's world

I am just a passerby of this
Tormented soul of many
Who walk smiling sadly
In their own epic story
Of this injustice world

Someone Else

A deep pain thriving within the
Shadows of a dust covered
Jaded stone
Puddles morphing from the
Throbbing blood into figures
Of my many imaginative yet
Tormentful creatures

The hour glass, fell over,
Shattering sand across the
Bathroom floor

Flooding across the floor,
Seeping into the cracks
In the walls
Such an unstoppable demon of
Chrono's delightful creature
To be some other lifeless machine,
A sweet thought

The dream to be of another soul
A different mind and body
To have perfection in his eyes

Over and over
Terror screams at me

Fear watches my every move
Death waits

What to do now
Where to go from here
A new life begs to live

Staggering to reach the door
Dreaming by the windowsill
I want to be another

In his eyes, an absolute deity
The mirror shows another side
My words rot my being
Thoughts of tomorrow
Crash and burn

This is not your lullaby to sing
Who are you? Another puzzler?
Stop staring at me
Like I am the freak

The Perfect Imperfect Lie

The adrenaline rush
A deep pit in your stomach
Your heart aching so much,
You wish you could cry

But you know once that
Glistening drop falls
It will turn into
A leaky faucet of 100 years

An imperfect waterfall,
Pouring out the dust

The devil's promise
For happiness, you take the
Golden token so willingly

Tripping on plushes of
Thorny duds,
You witness many
Picture-shattering memories
Screaming out never-to-be-
Mentioned again
Foggy memories

Cold as ice
To your-ever-so-comforting-self
Crueler than fire
To your support staff
Knowing your being will never
Be the same again

Punching holes in the wall
Scribing such hateful words,
Describing what thrives inside
Prepared to fight at
Chrono's satisfaction

Mad happiness laughs
Ever so wildly
There is no place for me,
Revenge will not make
The pain go away

Gentle comforting oracles
Flutter swiftly,
Whispering that soon it will
Disappear until the next round

Your faint twinkling stars,
Showing the story
Without sound

Allowing many to see the
Glimpses of the joy,
The cruelness, the hurt and love

Another nemesis has captured
Your soulless heart

Foreign Affairs

A body tanned
Like a bronzed god
So dedicated to learning

Bed sex hair going
This way and that way
Intense glowing jaded gems
Pinocchio-faced
In a older mannish way

Plain t-shirts made sexy upon
His lean muscular body
Such a handsome gentleman
Without knowledge of it

Perfect eye candy for the
Occasional window shopper
One glance will not do,
A full stare is needed to
Appreciate the beauty
In such a civilized creature

Behind that glorious mask is
Something much deeper than
The average horny jackass,
A kinder simpler innocent child
Each movement made, every
Wrinkle of his skin
So perfectly done

Perfect in every way,
Perfect in body,
Perfect in mind,
Perfect in soul,

Perfect in steaming beauty
Glistening sweet sweat so pure
And an innocent man

Strawberry Gashes

The devil knows her
He lights a tiny candle
For every one she does
To herself
She is going solo

The music in her head is
Blasting deadly tunes
Gently shutting her eyes,
She sees him
He is there, right there standing
In front of her
With outstretched arms,
Begging to hold her

A halo of clouds fog her vision
In a few lonely moments
Will come the rainstorm again

Death is life
Living is dying

Her emotions are so mixed up,
That she does not know
What is real

To the left is her rusty knight,
To the right is the devil
Yet lo' and behold,
Mirages mimic shadows
Devil here, devil there,
Devil all around
There is no escaping

Lying in front of her is
Her possible future

She decorates her body
With the ceremonial tattoos
Blood drips from all over

Strawberry gashes smile evil as
They keep secret their stories
The devil prepares to
Save the ashes

Galloping fast and long
The rusty knight leans
Over and grabs her

He takes her away,
Hoping that someday
He can take away her pain

She lives to die another day
In the arms of a devil

Unholy Horror

Elle ressemble a baise
N'est-ce pas?
Does she not look Fucked?

In the mist of her timelessness,
Faint splashes of deadly salt
Trenches upon the
Soft linens that cloak her
Anguished awareness has
Embodied itself deep

Curiosity from her fellow
Crowd of insolence
Betrayed her in fascination
Dangerously, the throbbing
Snarl of fear decides
To drift away

Looking gravely noble,
A soft murmur rise from the
Hollow decay of dead eyes
Aimless progress of running in
Fear through death's many traps

Her disappearing being rising
Like a memory from the solely
Fought dust cloud,
In a matter of freezed moments,
Her shameful innocence will be
Doomed from stifled cries

Quiet stones, gleam of the
Untold rendered senseless life
No more will she search for life,
Now her nostrils fill with death,

The ever so sweetness of the
Echoing chalky-state-of-mind
One more damned soul floats in
Eternity at the crossing
Of the threshold

The air there, absorbing all the
Sound and much of the Hateful light

Roughed coolness that aches in
Her desolate bones
Revive hand-held captured
Sparkles of dust
Cruel simplicity of her life
Drained from her now forever

Sweet Lies

In the somber of silence
I lie there upon rocky cliffs
Slowly my subconscious drifts
Into my being and
Asleep is my conscious
Dreams of early years
Come to be

Over there, in the distance,
A sorrowed violin
Strings out beautifully
Gentle as the soft plunder of a
Trotting horse,
The keys are stroked

Again I remember those
Heartfelt feelings from
Old memories

Scared to look behind,
I feel the presence of your being
The shadows overlook my body,
Still as stone

Brightly, a light tears a hole
Throughout the blissful Serenade
Everything stops only for
A moment but it feels
Like an eternity

Raining bullets of fury tear
Through my soft skin
Still standing with
Many bullet holes,
I see the shadows that
Were once behind me,
Coming to be in front of me

Their faces, blacker than the
Bottom of an empty well
They seem to stare, watching intently
as I fall timelessly
To the checkered-tiled floor

My fall sounds like a hundred
Trees chopped down,
Landing hard
I make no sound only
But a little groan

There, on the floor, I die
Drowning in my own sea of
Gushing blood
Sweet lies I have created

When A Rose Cries

Thorns of prickly emotions
Scar the dark green vine
That has grown over but
Around the tombstone of
Another lost soul beckoning
Redemption

Tonight, as the moon shines
Over the long ago buried
Hollow souls in the graveyard,
The rose becomes moonstruck

Moonstruck for the beloved,
Whose soul that has found
No rest

Deep crimson drops of
Decaying tears stream down the
Engraved letters R I P

A pool of tears collect Somewhere
Over the freshly buried grave
The overturned soil, moist with
The fallen rose tears

As the soul has
Long ago departed,
The body remains a decaying
Pile of worms

When the moon is
Full and glowing
A rose can be heard crying,
Mourning its lost

Thursday's Child

Snowy whiteness reaches out
Clasping within its stem-vines

Your soft plushes of
Blushing shadows
Confessing deep secrets,
All the red lies and
The watery truth
It is a comforting lie to believe
In something mystic

Striding along the cloudy grayness,
Wondering but
Never looking for heart

The path has become so unclear
But home is not near anymore

Sweet burdens fill your bags of
Hopes and purses full of dreams

Roll out the carts filled with
Your every black rose
Watch as they lower the
Silver-lined coffin, listen to the
Silence of mourning

Does the music not sound so
Weary of dreadfulness?
They are singing your song

Dance while you still can
Follow your footsteps into
Your many closets full of
Infinite skeletons
Swear to secrecy of our souls

Here come the pall bearers
All painted in fake sorrow
Gleaming with chasing misery
Justice will not be done

Flee in horror, look back and
You will damn yourself
To this world
6 feet above from the rotting,
Worm-infested dull glassy box

The rainy fog screams
"Times up" as the coffin lid Slams!

My Now Myth Existence

Reaped from my possession
The entity of being, stolen

Confined to four walls
Restricted from all my stones
Forbidden of the hold,
Tight grip on happiness

My rights to be,
Torn and shredded

The seraph flies over me,
Waiting and watching
Champions of my belongings,
The crows and ravens

Sweet black feathers shower me
These black figures, they laugh
When I laugh

In my mourning, they too, cry

Mankind's measured passing,
Drag on as they please

The nights become long,
The days, sometimes long,
Sometimes short
The weeks become months
Alas, months therefore
Become years
And years turn into eternity
Each second longer than the last

As I lay here
Slowly dying,
Slowly rotting away
My happy place has died
And crumbled

The hope was once here,
But now gone
Chunks of my heart
Has turned to fire
Disappearing into nothing

Is there no savior who dare
Come to my rescue?
Oh savior, savior
Where could thou be?

A Lost Teen

A child trapped within
Confusion making a mess
In the crowded space
Choices everywhere

So innocent, so precious,
So easily broken
The clothes never fit
Starving from loneliness

Embarrassed to come out and
Face the world
Untamed angel-soft hair
In stringy knots

Freezing cold inside
But does not know
Where to go for warmth
Small grumbling stomachs
Ache for food
This child is not a child

Another lost teen in society's

"How To Be Beautiful So That Everyone Will Notice You" book

This teen has no where to go
No place to call home anymore
Abandoned by society,
Left to wander the streets
Once again

But alas, the teen does have
A home, a warm bed to sleep in,
Clothes in its closet and a family

But this home and family,
Never was perfect
Another broken home falling
Apart again
Home sweet home,
Does not exist anymore

Yelling, screaming, fighting
Words destroying
The teen's self-image
Actions hurting the teen

Tears flooding the house in
3 feet deep of bitter-salty water
Everyday

Laughter seldom comes around
Anymore

Sadness lingers in every room
Pain and agony have soaked the
Walls dark blue

Every night, the teen looks up at
The stars and wishes it could be
Someone else

Someone whose happy

No matter how many
Birthday wishes and
Shooting star wishes,
The wish never came true

About the Author

A small town girl, next door type, she was a military brat before birth. Her inspirations are Edgar Allan Poe, Beethoven, Chopin, and Vincent Price. From sea to shining sea, she has traveled the world and peered deep within her mind. And found these words before you. Traveler by nature, writer by heart.